Never Picked First For Playtime

Dustin Brookshire

Harbor Editions
Small Harbor Publishing

Never Picked First For Playtime
Copyright © 2023 DUSTIN BROOKSHIRE
All rights reserved.

Cover art by Jen Stein Hauptmann
Cover design by Jen Stein Hauptmann and Allison Blevins
Book layout by Allison Blevins and Hannah Martin

NEVER PICKED FIRST FOR PLAYTIME
DUSTIN BROOKSHIRE
ISBN 978-1-957248-10-3
Harbor Editions,
an imprint of Small Harbor Publishing

for Denise

Foreword

I started writing poems featuring Barbie in the late 1980s. Back then, some literary magazine editors rejected the poems, advising me that writing about a flimsy pop culture icon might produce timely—but certainly not timeless—poems. Over the years, I also worried that the poems from *Kinky* would fall away to obscurity or need detailed footnotes to inform a reader. I thought, perhaps, Bratz dolls would take over. These sassy dolls were all the rage in 2001, but even at the height of their popularity, they still only had 40% of the fashion doll market, with Barbie holding steady at 60%. Mattel (Barbie's manufacturer) tied up MGA (Bratz's manufacturer) in a lawsuit claiming that the eyes of Bratz dolls looked too much like Barbie's. After a series of redesigns and fluctuation in sales, Bratz collector dolls are now sold only on Amazon while Barbie is still going strong.

Both Barbie and Bratz are still blamed for contributing to the sexualization of young girls, perfectionism, and issues around race. Writers address these issues in an exquisite anthology *Mondo Barbie* published in 1993 by St. Martin's Press. The multi-genre collection, edited by Rick Peabody and Lucinda Ebersole, was actually printed on pink paper. I address these issues in the poems in *Kinky* (Orchises Press, 1997). Now, fast forward twenty-five years later. Dustin has kept the pink flame of Barbie poems going. He even invited me to co-edit a special issue of *Limp Wrist* (March 2022) dedicated to the doll.

And now we celebrate the publication of Dustin Brookshire's *Never Picked First For Playtime*. Dustin's sensibility is decidedly camp—with lines like "The boys grow up . . . to free their inner Barbie" and titles like "Barbie Watches Golden Girls." But the collection is also fraught with up-to-the-minute political references, imagining Barbie's relationship to HIV travel bans, Covid and anti-vaxxers, MAGA voters, marriage equality, and whiteness. Dustin is not afraid to go there, using Barbie as a vehicle to respond to our fraught cultural moment. He is fearless in his accusations but also tender towards the poems themselves.

Baudelaire writes that playing with dolls marks the beginning of abstraction and imagination—and, of course, possibility. Dustin's poems are lively, conjuring more than just worlds. Rilke likens dolls to God, as both "have become famous mainly by not speaking to us." Dustin's poems often feel like secular prayers. He demonstrates the wisdom to interrogate pop culture and the culture at large. He also works in a literary tradition with mischievous riffs on Maggie Smith and Margaret Atwood poems. As I proudly pass the torch to Dustin (in this case, a "Solo in the Spotlight" Barbie), I know she's in good hands.

—Denise Duhamel, January 2023

Contents

Pandemic Barbie / 13

COVID-19 Barbie / 14

Lot's Wife Barbie / 15

Salome Barbie Speaks With A Mattel Historian / 16

Blue Lives Matter Barbie / 17

Lesbian Barbie / 18

Homophobic Barbie / 19

PSA From Lesbian Barbie / 20

MAGA Barbie / 21

Red Lobster Barbie / 23

Susan Collins Barbie / 24

Anti-Vaxxer Barbie / 25

Colonoscopy Barbie / 26

HIV Barbie / 27

Barbie's Guilty Pleasure / 29

Barbie's Realization / 30

Barbie Watches The Golden Girls / 31

Barbie's Funeral / 32

Limited Edition Good Bones Barbie / 33

Afterward / 35

Notes / 37

Acknowledgements / 39

Never Picked First For Playtime

Pandemic Barbie
after Denise Duhamel's "Antichrist Barbie"

She sits inside her Barbie Malibu Dreamhouse—
a socialite waiting on her assistant.
Her body yearns to be dressed
by little girls, but especially those little boys
who bring the glitz and glamour.
Mothers debate—let the dolls sit for 2 to 3 days
post play date or wipe them down with Lysol.
Barbie doesn't have COVID, cry little girls,
and little boys, who in secret, love her.
The boys grow up to cinch their waists,
sissy their walk, balk at lace front wigs,
leave families behind, free their inner Barbie,
grow up to be men thankful
one blue pill a day prevents at least one virus.

COVID-19 Barbie

No one removes her from the box.

Lot's Wife Barbie

Mattel told her not to look
back once she left the factory.

We know how that ended.

Never picked first for playtime,
she's a lifesaver when a recipe
calls for a pinch of salt.

Salome Barbie Speaks With A Mattel Historian

I understand
Ken the Baptist
holds a grudge,
but after all these years—
the gifts of super glue—
I only see Ken the Martyr.

My legendary dance
wasn't that legendary.
I don't have joints!
March of the seven veils
is more like it,
but that doesn't sell
femme fatale.

I don't remember
what Ken said
to anger Mother.
If I'm being honest,
he's always been cute—
for a religious Ken.

Tell me,
who hasn't regretted
a decision made solely
to please their mother?

Blue Lives Matter Barbie

Lesbian Barbie

Plastic body to plastic body
in the toy box
with all the other Barbies.
She's horrified when her arm
that was left reaching for the sky
is now up Christmas Barbie's ball gown.
(She respects consent.)

People think she's good
with power tools,
could build a deck or add a room
to the Barbie Dreamhouse,
but she's never held a drill.
(She can't!)

Lesbian Barbie is envious
of Made to Move Baseball Player Barbie's
22 joints—some in the neck,
wrists, torso, and hips—
that allow for, as Mattel says,
*Lots of flexibility and an incredible
range of movement.* She knows
with joints she'd be a player,
hopes to join Mattel's baseball team,
at least one Baseball Player Barbie
has to be a lesbian too.

Homophobic Barbie

She didn't picket when marriage equality passed,
only asked, *How do you know who the bride is?*
When SCOTUS ruled on workplace discrimination,
she was silent on Facebook, but asked Ken,
Do people really get fired for being gay?
Homophobic Barbie will tell you
she's had an owner or two turn gay.
(Technically, it was her owner's brothers.)
She knew one was gay when he made Q-tips
into hair rollers. The other
instigated arguments between her and Ken.
Ken had never questioned why he wasn't allowed
to drive the Barbie Convertible across the living room.
Homophobic Barbie *loves the sinner, hates the sin.*
She isn't sure two dads or two moms
create the best environment for a child
but shows up for the wedding.
She isn't missing an open bar
or chance to do the Electric Slide
in pink heels with her sister Skipper.
After her third glass of champagne,
Homophobic Barbie explains to Skipper,
Remember, in the beginning,
Mattel created Barbie and Ken, not Ben and Ken.

PSA From Lesbian Barbie

Scissoring is a cisgender male construct.

MAGA Barbie

She could be from Georgia, Florida, South Carolina,
Alabama, or any state that voted red in 2016.
Little girls never pick her.
Mothers make the purchase,
bribe their daughters to pose with Barbie,
wear a matching MAGA hat.
Mothers post pictures
on Twitter, Instagram, and Facebook.
#MAGAWomen
#WomenForTrump
#TrumpGirlsBreakTheInternet

MAGA Ken isn't sold separately,
Barbie's instruction sheet
explains a strong MAGA family
is led by a man. Barbie and Ken
are married, why else would
they be so close in that box?

After the photo shoot,
mother's quickly trash Barbie's box.
Some daughters notice
Barbie's logo isn't her signature cursive,
pink isn't pantone pink,
it's M-A-T-E-L-L instead of M-A-T-T-E-L
on the bottom of the box.
Girls Google, quickly discover
the Trump campaign launched MAGA Barbie
after Mattel announced Barbie Campaign Team Giftset:
a campaign manager, fundraiser, voter,
and a black presidential candidate.
Barbie Giftset includes a link to a downloadable

voting ballot, "I'm a Future Voter!" sticker,
and "You Can Be Anything" activity sheets.
Daughters prefer these items to the 5% discount code
for *Art of the Deal*, prefer Barbie Giftset
over MAGA Barbie and Ken who remind
them of what they don't want to be.

Red Lobster Barbie

will fuck you up
if you get between
her and her basket
of cheddar biscuits.

Susan Collins Barbie

Mattel strategists
planned a limited 10-year run.
Twenty plus years later,
she is still for sale.

Anti-Vaxxer Barbie

jokes with best friend
Anti-Masker Barbie—
the only MMR she wants
is men, money, and Reagan.

Her cousin Jazzie
has a coworker
who knows someone
whose sister
knows someone
that stepped on a nail,
got a Tetanus shot—
now he's Autistic.

It's true, she says,
*Jenny McCarthy almost
interviewed the mom
for one of her books.*
Anti-Vaxxer Barbie idolizes
Jenny, shero of their movement.

Anti-Vaxxer Barbie tweets fans weekly:
Babes, vaccine free is microchip free.
Big Brother ain't tracking this gal.
Her truth is her mini-pink cross to bear.

Colonoscopy Barbie

*Will children develop a fixation
if an anus is her only orifice?*
asked a Mattel strategist.
*The list of what will end
up her ass is endless,*
said a senior strategist.

Colonoscopy Barbie
existed only as a discussion.

A secret kept until this poem.

HIV Barbie

Barbie doesn't understand why Cuba & Belize
require HIV testing for visitors staying
longer than 3 months. Her celebrity status
may not help her in Egypt,
non-nationals with HIV may be deported.
Aruba won't grant work permits to anyone positive.
Barbie gripes to Ken:
Who wants to go to Cuba?
Belize! Well, what do they have to offer?
The pyramids aren't all that,
and I can do a photo shoot on any damn beach!

Barbie can't comprehend the fuss.
She doesn't worry about bleeding cuts
or scrapes or sharing needles.
(*Just say no to drug*s, Barbie shrugs.)
She doesn't even have blood
nor openings for necessity or pleasure.
No orifice means none—ask Ken,
that fact often makes him blue.

Her box comes with an information sheet
dispelling HIV transmission myths:
It's safe to comb Barbie's hair.
It's safe to take a bath with Barbie.
Meds are not included.
Barbie wipes her forehead.
How would she take the pills anyway?

Mattel never placed her in circulation.
Tucked away deep in a Mattel closet,
Infectious Disease Doctor Ken takes care of her,

though her body will never age.
She doesn't have to worry about routine blood work
or telling friends, family, or fans she's positive.
They'd only ask how she contracted HIV.

Barbie's Guilty Pleasure

After Barbie is buzzed
on Dom Pérignon
or Grey Goose dirty martinis
with three blue cheese stuffed olives,
she slips a few houses down
from her Dreamhouse,
hair pulled up in a bun,
pink scarf wrapped around her head,
wears Livhò Retro vintage narrow cat eye sunglasses
even though the sun's been down for hours,
to wait for Lyft
under the name Barbara.
(Barbie doesn't drink and drive!)
She enjoys the wait
in the Taco Bell drive-through
reminiscing about those first years
before she was a household name
until she hears the driver order
a Nacho BellGrande,
Cheesy Gordita Crunch,
and a Baja Blast without a straw.
(Barbie cares about sea turtles!)
She tips the driver extra
for a longer route home.
She enjoys her food in peace,
stops where she won't be noticed
to trash the evidence.

Barbie's Realization

after Margaret Atwood

You fit onto me
Like a shoe onto a foot

A mini pink stiletto heel
A gnawed right foot

Barbie Watches The Golden Girls

She won't retire to Miami,
open a pizza stand by the beach,
enter an all-night dance-a-thon,
start an unauthorized Elvis fan club.
She won't enjoy cheesecake
in the middle of the night
while solving problems.
(Thanks Mattel privilege!)
Ken says she'd be a total Blanche.
You're a total Stan, fuck boy,
Barbie mumbles under her breath.
She knows she'd be a Rose.
(Barbie's so goddamn loveable!)
When the credits roll,
Barbie tries not to think about
the truth of it all—
even with all the fans,
the Mattel universe
won't allow her
that kind of sisterhood.

Barbie's Funeral

A little girl tucks Barbie in a shoe box,
fake cries, *She's gone—*
like grandma.
Her slightly older brother,
thanks to a recent movie,
points to the pool,
suggests a Viking send off.
Quickly dismissed, her brother
finds his mother's hand shovel,
digs a grave beside their swing set.
The little girl plucks rose petals
to scatter over the grave,
but her brother's hand tires
after ten stabs into the dirt.
Their mother yells,
Time for lunch, from inside.
The little girl knocks off the lid,
pulls Barbie out while screaming,
Surprise! Barbie faked her death
like that lady on Days of Our Lives.

Limited Edition Good Bones Barbie

after Maggie Smith's "Good Bones"

Life isn't short when you're plastic.
It takes a thousand years to decompose.
Mattel tells Barbie:
Think of all the delicious ways you'll live,
collecting centuries like charms on a bracelet.
Mattel keeps the truth from Barbie:
For every Barbie that is loved,
kept safe, passed down
generation to generation,
there is a Barbie melted
on a stove top, decapitated
by an older brother,
mauled by the family dog,
or forgotten on a playground.
Like any business seeking profit,
Mattel says what is needed
to keep the Barbie smile,
smiling: *You are famous,*
a name more recognizable
than Cher, Oprah, Madonna.
Millions of little girls want to be you.
They'll grow up to be women
who keep you on a shelf,
a shrine, a deity to worship.
Mattel never discloses—
even those people
sell Barbie on eBay
when the price is right.

Afterword

Anyone who knows me knows I'm a super fan of two Ds—Dolly and Denise. I discovered and fell in love with poetry through the work of Anne Sexton, but it is the poetry of Denise Duhamel that showed me I could write the type of poems I wanted to write. While a few high school teachers encouraged me to write poems, they also taught pop culture references don't have a place in poetry. Denise, queen of pop culture references, taught me otherwise. The narrative poems I studied in school left me uninterested, but Denise's narrative poems made me eager to move from line to line and inspired me to write my own. High school teachers taught us there wasn't anymore room for confessional poets and humor in poetry wasn't encouraged; however, Denise's poems showed me otherwise. I'd be remiss if I didn't thank my former college professor turned mentor and dear friend Beth Gylys for suggesting I read Denise's *Kinky* as well as for helping me strengthen my poetic voice.

Kinky is the book I recommend to everyone that shows poetry can be about anything. It's the book I pull from when people tell me they don't like poetry. It's the book that (actually!) taught me something about the "Dolly rumor mill"—thanks "Barbie in Therapy, Part II" for enlightening me about the rumor that Dolly is a lesbian. It's a book I keep a backup copy of in case my original is damaged beyond use. *Kinky* is a book I turn to again and again, and it never ceases to entertain and inspire me.

In 2007, when Dorianne Laux gave a lecture at the Palm Beach Poetry Festival on the importance of memorizing poems, it was "Antichrist Barbie" from *Kinky* I memorized. It was also at the 2007 Palm Beach Poetry Festival where I first met Denise. She was at the evening gala, and I pointed her out to a workshop peer who responded with, "You've brought her up in workshop. You have to meet her." In my true dramatic nature, I responded, "One cannot just approach Denise Duhamel." Well, one can just approach Denise. My workshop peer marched up to her, dragging me along, and asked: "Are you Denise Duhamel?" After Denise confirmed, my friend said, "You have to meet Dustin. He raved about you in workshop." Denise was generous with her time to talk poetry, *Kinky*, and more. She even waited for me to run to my car to get my copy of *Kinky* and autographed it. (I always take my favorite books to poetry conferences.) I still have that copy inscribed with: "*Kinky* is 10 this year!"

Kinky turned 25 on March 1, 2022, and this milestone birthday inspired me to write this chapbook of Barbie poems to honor Denise's groundbreaking collection.

Notes

The Blue Lives Matter movement began in 2014 as a countermovement to the Black Lives Matter movement. The key word is countermovement. If you espouse Blue Lives Matter, then you need to reflect deeply on your life and belief system because you're racist.

During a debate for her first US Senate campaign in 1996, Susan Collins was asked if she would support congressional term limits. Susan Collins answered with the following: *I do support term limits, and I have pledged that if I'm elected I will only serve two terms regardless of whether a term limits law constitutional amendment passes or not. Twelve years is long enough to be in public service, make a contribution, and then come home and let someone else take your place.* Susan Collins won the election in 1996. At the time of publication, Collins continues to serve as a US Senator from Maine.

The facts included in the first stanza of the chapbook version of "HIV Barbie" were taken from the 2019 UNAIDS report titled "Still Not Welcome: HIV-Related Travel Restrictions."

Acknowledgements

Many thanks to the following publications in which some of these poems, at times in earlier incarnations, originally appeared:

Panoply: "Pandemic Barbie"

Madness Muse Press: "Salome Barbie Speaks With A Mattel Historian" and "Colonoscopy Barbie"

Gulf Stream Magazine: "Lesbian Barbie"

Whale Road Review: "Homophobic Barbie"

Indolent Books' "What A Rough Beast" Series: "MAGA Barbie"

Indolent Books' "HIV Here & Now" Series: "HIV Barbie"

Alice Says Go Fuck Yourself: "Lot's Wife Barbie," "Barbie's Guilty Pleasure," and "Barbie's Realization"

South Florida Poetry Journal: "Limited Edition Good Bones Barbie"

Metro Weekly for republishing: "Homophobic Barbie" and "Limited Edition Good Bones Barbie"

Heartfelt gratitude to the Harbor Editions team and Allison Blevins for their dedication to poetry and giving this chapbook a home. Allison, you're a bright light in the poetry business; the universe was looking out for me when our life paths crossed.

Fiancé Chris, thank you for your love, friendship, and support. I'm lucky to have you in my life.

Beth, thank you for your feedback on many of these poems. Your candid feedback is always appreciated and was instrumental to the completion of this chapbook.

Thank you to the following friends for their support and/or feedback of/on my Barbie poems: Kim Addonizio and the 2022 spring workshop group, Julie E. Bloemeke, Emma Bolden, Chris Daughtrey, Aaron DeLee, Chris Dielmann, Ben Kline, and L.J. Sysko.

Finally, Denise, thank you for your friendship, support, and generosity. Most of all, thank you for *Kinky*.

Dustin Brookshire (he/him) is the author of the chapbooks *Never Picked First For Playtime* (Harbor Editions, 2023), *Love Most Of You Too* (Harbor Editions, 2021), and *To The One Who Raped Me* (Sibling Rivalry Press, 2012). He is the co-editor of *Let Me Say This: A Dolly Parton Poetry Anthology* (Madville Publishing, 2023) and the co-editor of a forthcoming forms anthology from Harbor Anthologies. His work has earned him both Pushcart and Best of the Net nominations, has appeared in numerous publications, and has been anthologized in *Divining Divas: 100 Gay Men on their Muses* (Lethe Press, 2012) and *The Queer South: LGBTQ Writes on the American South* (Sibling Rivalry Press, 2014). Dustin is the curator of the Wild & Precious Life Series, founder/editor of *Limp Wrist*, founding chapter president of the South Florida Poets (a chapter of the Florida State Poetry Association), program director for Reading Queer, and a founding member of FLAWN (Florida Local Artist & Writers Network). Find him online at dustinbrookshire.com.

www.ingramcontent.com/pod-product-compliance
Lightning Source LLC
Chambersburg PA
CBHW051704040426
42446CB00009B/1305